Portrait of
SALISBURY

TEXT BY SUE WALKER
WITH PHOTOGRAPHY BY STEVE DAY

HALSGROVE

First published in Great Britain in 2010

British Library Cataloguing-in-Publication Data
A CIP record for this title is available from the British Library

ISBN 978 0 85704 034 3

HALSGROVE
Halsgrove House,
Ryelands Industrial Estate,
Bagley Road, Wellington, Somerset TA21 9PZ
Tel: 01823 653777   Fax: 01823 216796
email: sales@halsgrove.com

Part of the Halsgrove group of companies
Information on all Halsgrove titles is available at: www.halsgrove.com

Printed and bound in Italy by Grafiche Flaminia

CONTENTS

The Matrons' College, just inside the North Gate, was completed in 1682. Bishop Seth Ward endowed it as an almshouse for ten clergy widows, and it is still an almshouse today.

The iconic spire, seen from near Hole Farm on the Old Road, Alderbury.

INTRODUCTION

Salisbury, or New Sarum, is the city of the spire. This impossibly tall, delicate, medieval icon is a landmark for travellers arriving from all points of the compass. Piercing the sky, and visible from up to twenty miles away, it soars above its unique, breathtaking cathedral. The cathedral, in turn, presides over the huge, tranquil haven of its idyllic, walled Close. Broad, verdant lawns are framed by an overwhelming array of architecturally and historically fascinating buildings.

Beyond the ethereal Close lies a medieval city with its large, vibrant Market Square and a street plan virtually unchanged since the chequers were symmetrically laid out over seven hundred years ago, when Old Sarum was abandoned by the Church. Ancient buildings and smile-inducing treasures and curiosities abound.

A very modest city by modern standards, Salisbury has an overwhelmingly friendly, market town feel to it. It is quite definitely a place to meet friends and relax. Parks and gardens, downland and rural water-meadows are just a short walk from the centre, and it sits at the confluence of five stunning rivers.

Important prehistoric monuments and gloriously sumptuous mansions stand within just five miles of this characterful, thriving city in southeast Wiltshire. Salisbury may be small but it boasts many superlatives, including a renowned international Arts Festival.

This is a very personal view of what makes Salisbury so special to visit or live in. Images that reflect all that is good about the city have been chosen.

ACKNOWLEDGEMENTS

Thanks are due to Richard Tambling, a great friend of Steve's, gifted
artist and photographer, for his dedication and hard work rushing about
Salisbury to get some wonderful images at Sue's request.
A huge thank you also to Tony Goddard for his tremendous support
throughout this project. It would never have happened without him.

Sue Walker, Farley

OLD SARUM,
THE FIRST SALISBURY

Salisbury began at Old Sarum, a large windswept site, just one mile north of the current city. There was a Neolithic settlement in the area, then an iron age hillfort. Known as Sorviodunum, it was the focus of a Roman road network, and later held and fortified by the Saxons. The ramparts were altered to house a Norman castle, a Bishop's palace and a cathedral, and a town grew up on and around the hill. Life there, under the Normans, was unsettled, with constant bickering between the clergy and the royal garrison. It was also wretchedly waterless so in 1219 Bishop Poore left the city and founded New Sarum in the fertile, sheltered river valley below. Old Sarum's cathedral was demolished in 1331 and its stone was taken to Salisbury to construct the Close wall. The site was gradually abandoned and was officially declared uninhabited by the nineteenth century .

Old Sarum today dominates the road to Amesbury, and towers above the Avon valley. The earth ramparts, extensive foundations of that first cathedral, and substantial remains of the Norman motte and bailey castle are fascinating. There are also breathtaking, panoramic views of "New Sarum" to the south, and Salisbury Plain to the north.

The royal palace with the Great Tower beyond.

9

NEW SARUM, TODAY'S SALISBURY

Today's Salisbury was a "new town", purpose-built on an empty, level site in the valley below Old Sarum. The medieval city was designed as a symmetrical grid of "chequers", next to the new cathedral in its spacious Close, and a huge central market place was created to ensure Salisbury's commercial importance.

Bishop Poore gained permission to build the new city in 1219 and laid the three foundation stones of the cathedral in 1220. A royal charter in 1227 allowed a weekly market on Tuesdays, and an annual fair, and a further charter in 1315 added an extra weekly market on Saturdays. The markets and the fair continued for the next seven hundred years and are still popular today.

The cathedral and its Close are utterly sublime, and Wiltshire's only city, despite its growth, has retained much of its medieval character and a wealth of rewarding features in the twenty-first century.

The Close in winter.

View from the south, in a glorious autumn setting. The Chilmark stone can look breathtakingly golden on some days, and a sad grey on others.

THE CATHEDRAL CHURCH OF THE BLESSED VIRGIN MARY

Almost all British cathedrals reflect several different architectural styles because they were built gradually over centuries, with repeated additions and remodellings. Salisbury cathedral is unique in that it was completed, including the ornamental West Front, the Cloisters and Chapter House, in a single generation, giving it an aesthetic unity of design. Even the tower and spire were completed less than a hundred years after the foundation stones were laid. The cathedral is a uniquely pure example of Early English architecture, simple and elegant. The use of soft, cream Chilmark stone, and dark, hard, polished Purbeck marble adds to the cathedral's simplicity.

The slender, octagonal spire, rising to the stupendous height of 404 feet, is the tallest medieval structure in the world. Sir Christopher Wren recorded that it was "out of true", and now, after seven hundred and fifty years it leans 29 inches southwest. It is definitely Salisbury's crowning glory.

Salisbury boasts the largest and earliest Cloisters of any English cathedral. Its central garth has magnificent cedars of Lebanon, planted to celebrate Queen Victoria's accession to the throne. The Chapter House is one of the best examples of Gothic architecture anywhere in England.

The aesthetically pleasing cathedral from the south-west corner of the Close.

14

The Cathedral was built in just thirty eight years, being completed by 1258.

Some thirty years later the tower was heightened…

…and an audacious spire, weighing 6,500 tons, was added to give the Cathedral we know today. The additional weight caused the four supporting piers to bend, so that buttresses and strainer arches were needed urgently, to prevent the edifice from toppling.

The magnificent West Front, wide and imposing,
has tiers of niches filled with statues of bishops,
saints, angels, kings, martyrs and prophets.
A few are medieval, some are very new, but all
have been cleaned and restored in recent years.

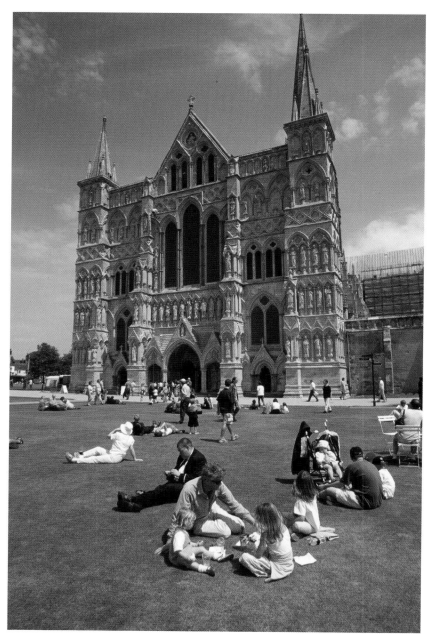

Seven hundred years of weathering and pollution
have taken their toll on the soft Chilmark
limestone of the cathedral. Newly carved statues,
like this exquisite angel, have been placed in
empty niches on the West Front.

Looking west, from the Nave, through the choir to the Chapel of the Holy Trinity and All Saints.

Looking up, from the Nave, one appreciates the elegance of the vaulted ceiling. The muted, understated colours complement the simplicity of the curves.

The sleek new font, with calm reflections and flowing water, has graced the Nave since 2008. It was created by William Pye to celebrate the cathedral's 750th anniversary, and is the largest working font in any British cathedral.

© Richard Tambling

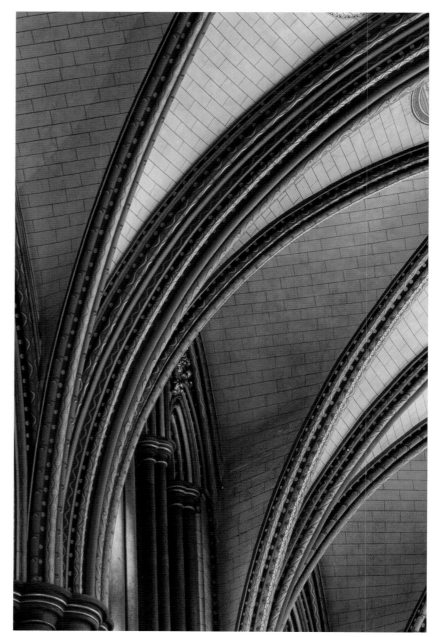

A detail from the thought-provoking 1980 "Prisoners of Conscience" window by Gabriel Loire, of Chartres.
Its rich, vibrant colours glow when lit by a rising sun.

Attending the Advent Service "From Darkness into Light" is a truly uplifting, magical experience. The congregation waits silently in utter darkness, which is slowly transformed as candle-bearers process, lighting several hundred candles. Dim lighting and flickering shadows echo what it must have been like in medieval times, and the angelic sound of the choir raises the hairs on the back of one's neck.

The medieval windlass, at the base of the spire, was used to raise the stones needed to construct the spire. It is still usable and can lift almost a ton.

The Cathedral Plumbery now houses a shop and atmospheric dining restaurant, giving unusual views of the spire through its glass roof.

The fourteenth-century clock is the oldest working clock in Europe. It has no clockface, but simply strikes the hour.

21

The thirteenth-century, octagonal Chapter House is pure Gothic. Ample windows ensure that the building is full of light.

Left: *The fifteenth-century cathedral library stands above the east walk of the Cloister.*

The wonderfully-delicate fan vaulting of the Chapter House radiates from a tall, slender central pillar of polished Purbeck marble.

The Chapter House contains the best of the four surviving originals of the Magna Carta.
A bronze statue commemorates its signing by King John at Runnymede.

The Chapter House has a medieval frieze of exquisite carved stories from Genesis, including Noah planting his vineyard.

26

THE CLOSE

Few cathedrals enjoy a setting like Salisbury's. The Close, at eighty acres, is the largest cathedral close in the country. The cathedral itself is surrounded by five acres of smooth lawns, then a low, medieval graveyard wall.

Beyond, the perimeter of mansions, cottages and halls forms the perfect backdrop to a quite sublime scene. Finally, the Close is shielded from the brash, bustling modern world outside by a sweep of the River Avon and by high medieval walls built from stone taken from Old Sarum.

Walking into the Close through the main High Street gate is like stepping back in time. There are many remarkable examples of Georgian and other complementary architecture, along West, North and Bishop's Walks and around Choristers' Green, and even medieval architecture can be discovered.

Properties on the west side of the Close have large, well-stocked, mature gardens with the crystal clear River Avon as their western boundary. Some gardens are open to the public in summer, allowing visitors to enjoy their unique setting. Originally intended for the cathedral's secular canons, many of the opulent residences around the Close are now leased by the Church as private residences. Several are museums or schools.

The Close remains a calm oasis, somewhat aloof from the city outside. Its three public access gates, set in the impenetrable Close walls, are still locked every night by Close constables, and remain closed from 11.30 p.m. until 7.00 a.m.

The lawns were added in 1780, to replace a medieval belltower and a graveyard full of tombstones.

The bronze "Walking Madonna" was cast by Elisabeth Frink in 1981. Rather gaunt, she stands in the Close, loved and hated, but compelling and much photographed.

29

View from the northeast, showing the medieval graveyard wall, built with stone brought from Old Sarum.

A splendid eighteenth-century mansion, the Walton Canonry, has been home to famous people such as Isaac Walton (son of the celebrated angler), artist Rex Whistler and author Leslie Thomas.

Arundells, on West Walk, incorporates parts of a medieval canonry. A beautiful formal garden of two acres leads back to the banks of the Avon behind the pleasing, symmetrical house. It was the home of former Prime Minister Sir Edward Heath, until his death in 2005, and is now open to the public.

Left: *The King's House is a marvellous, historic building and the home of the Salisbury and South Wiltshire Museum. It has fascinating galleries full of local history, archaeology and culture, and also holds excellent exhibitions.*

The Medieval Hall is elegantly proportioned with a fine timber-framed roof and original central hearth. Groups can watch a "Discover Salisbury" film show in this magnificent setting.

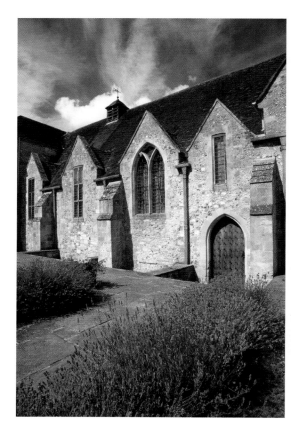

The Medieval Hall is also the oldest building in the Close. It was the banqueting great hall of the Old Deanery, residence of Deans from the thirteenth century until 1922. It has been lovingly restored and is a great venue for a wide variety of private and public events.

Braybrooke House and Wren Hall lie on the west side of Choristers' Green.

Left: *Hemingsby, once yet another medieval canonry, has a fourteenth-century wing and fifteenth-century hall. A major repair needed some three hundred years ago has left it with the appearance of two very different, separate houses.*

The fourteenth-century wing of Hemingsby, showing tile and flint construction, and a lovely window. © Richard Tambling

The National Trust's genteel Mompesson House is a splendid Queen Anne town house.
The eighteenth-century house, its walled garden and small tearoom are a superb destination on a summer's day.

The North, or High Street, Gate once had a portcullis. It is still locked every night.

A statue of King Edward VII stands in a small niche above the gate, on the Close side.

An architectural miscellany on North Walk.

Sarum College, on North Walk, houses a Theological College and library.

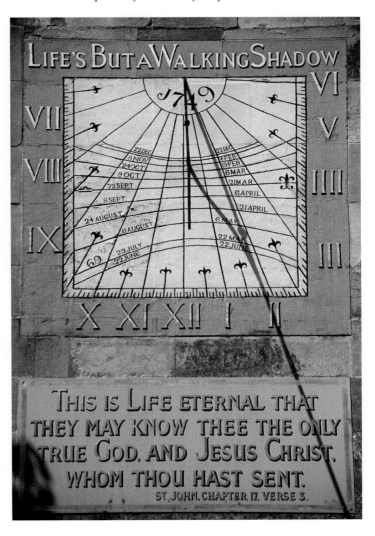

The sundial on the wall of Malmesbury House records the month and day as well as the time.

The king allowed the Dean and Chapter to protect themselves in 1327 by building "an embattled wall of stone" around the Close. Saint Ann's Gate, in the east wall, had a chapel built over it, which then became a room of Malmesbury House. Handel once gave a concert there. The wall, and gate, certainly reflect their medieval origins.

Inset: *The Royal Arms of Her Majesty Queen Elizabeth II adorns the gateway.*

Cottages on Bishop's Walk, east of the cathedral graveyard.

The former Bishop's Palace has some medieval features of Bishop Poore's original 1220 home.
It is now the Cathedral School, which was founded at Old Sarum in 1091.

THE MARKET SQUARE, ROWS AND CHEQUERS

A place to shop, bump into or meet with friends, the Market Square remains an integral part of life in Salisbury.

The Market Square was originally more than twice its current, capacious size. The market's success contributed to the decline of Old Sarum and Wilton. Stalls were replaced by permanent buildings and gradual "market in-filling" and encroachment occurred, to give the Rows we see today. Their names, including Butcher, Fish, Oatmeal, and Ox Rows, reflect their origins. Many of the buildings have changed use and physical appearance repeatedly over time. The Market Square had, and will undoubtedly continue to have, numerous "fashionable" makeovers.

The new city's wide streets were laid out as an almost regular grid on a greenfield site. The areas between them became the "chequers", named after inns, houses or important people. Twenty one chequers include the evocative Antelope, Three Swans, Cross Keys, White Hart, Black Horse, Three Cups, Trinity, Mitre, Gores and Swayne's. A large part of the medieval layout is intact.

The Market Square has been the beating heart of the city for almost 800 years. It has gained colourful, Mediterranean-style pavement cafés and floral creations in recent years.

The market now has lots of stalls with modern fare such as delicious olives and organic produce.

The three day Michaelmas Fair, held in the Market Square every October,
has been entertaining people in various ways since it began in 1227.

50

Left: *The rather noble, classically proportioned Guildhall stands at the southern edge of the Market. It was built in the late 1700s as a gift from the local nobleman, the Earl of Radnor.*

Right: *Blue Boar Row, with its eclectic mix of buildings, still marks the original north boundary of the medieval market place. Debenham's department store stands on the site of the medieval Boar Inn, and its restaurant incorporates some of the Inn's original features.*

Queen Street still forms the eastern boundary of the original medieval market place. From Cross Keys House down past the Cross Keys shopping mall to William Russel's House lies a wealth of fascinating architectural treasures.

51

Left: *A stroll into the modern Cross Keys shopping mall off Queen Street, takes one past a crooked, seventeenth-century staircase that once led up to the gallery of the "Plume of Feathers" inn.*

Right: *William Russel's house, on Queen Street, is wrongly known as the House of John A' Port. It is a remarkable, well preserved timber-framed house from around 1310, behind a later façade. Parts of its medieval structure can be seen inside.*

Below: *Detail of the House of John A' Port on Queen Street.*

Ye·House·of·John·A·Port·   Three·Lyon·Chequer·

53

An area of exposed medieval wattle and daub and stunning medieval roof timbers in the House of John A' Port.
Both images © Richard Tambling

Butcher Row eventually became the southern boundary of Salisbury's Market Square.

Butcher Row and Fish Row are lovely examples of "market infill". Their names reflect the trades that moved from market stalls to permanent buildings. Ox, Oatmeal and Ironmonger Rows are other examples.

Number 33 Butcher Row dates from around 1520. An ugly façade was removed to reveal the original worn and weathered oak timber framing, now once again on show.

© Richard Tambling

The hexagonal Poultry Cross is a well-known landmark. It is the only survivor of four such market crosses from the fifteenth century. The ornate structures above the balustrade were added in Victorian times.

A fine set of historic buildings stands on Minster Street, opposite the Poultry Cross.

The Haunch of Venison Inn is five-hundred-years old, with vestiges of its medieval origins. It is small and intimate, with a tiny snug, wildly sloping floors and intimate atmosphere. Its popular restaurant sits, at a jaunty angle, over the jeweller's shop next door.

The popular public library was once a grand, bustling, covered Market House, with its own (very short!) railway line to Salisbury's mainline station. It stands in front of the Cheesemarket, by the Market Square. Its façade was described, when finished in 1859, as in the form of an ancient Roman basilica!

Below: The partly pedestrianised High Street has several interesting buildings. This fourteenth-century row of timber-framed and jettied houses is currently a restaurant.

The apparently ancient, symbolic ram of 51 High Street by the North Gate is actually from the early twentieth century, when Stonehenge Woollen Industries occupied the building. Certainly, much of Salisbury's wealth came from the wool trade.

© Richard Tambling

Below: The upper storeys of the medieval George Inn survive. Oliver Cromwell and Samuel Pepys stayed there, and Shakespeare and his players performed in its courtyard. That courtyard now forms part of Old George Mall shopping mall.

The Town, or Bishop's, Mill, upstream of Fisherton Bridge, stands on the site of a mill noted in the Domesday Book. A working mill, rebuilt several times, it is currently a popular watering hole, known simply as "The Mill".

© Richard Tambling

62

Saint Thomas's Square, next to St Thomas's church, is a pleasant, sheltered spot to stop for tea and cakes. All the buildings here are more examples of "market infill". © Richard Tambling

St Thomas's church was founded at the same time as the city, for the cathedral builders to worship in, but much of today's church dates from the fifteenth century.

A slate sundial, commissioned by Salisbury's University of the Third Age Group, can be seen high on a wall in the passage linking Saint Thomas's Square to the Cheesemarket.

The simple but atmospheric church contains a remarkable "doom" painting around and over the chancel arch. This was painted in the fifteenth century but was whitewashed over and "lost" for three hundred years. It was then rediscovered and restored in the 1800s and is now the largest surviving "doom" painting in England.

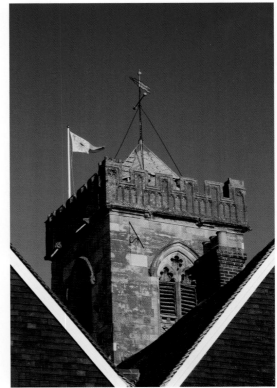

St Thomas's church tower detail.

Salisbury has a good number of interesting inns from the fifteenth century onwards.
The New Inn on New Street, often bedecked in flowers, is just a short stroll from the cathedral.

Church House, east of Crane Bridge, is a complex of buildings that functioned as the City Workhouse in the seventeenth and eighteenth centuries. The oldest part was built as the house of a wealthy merchant over five hundred years ago.

Crane Bridge has spanned the Avon since the middle ages, although it has been much altered and widened. It links the city centre to Queen Elizabeth Gardens, and it is one of life's pleasures to stand on the bridge and watch fat brown trout shimmering in the current.

The fifteenth-century, timber-framed Pheasant Inn on Salt Lane incorporates…

© Richard Tambling

…the seventeenth-century Shoemakers' Hall, now part of the "gastropub".

© Richard Tambling

No visit to Salisbury is complete without a peek inside the unusual Odeon Cinema! Originally built for John Halle in 1495, a cinema was tacked onto the back in 1929. The facade is "mock" medieval and the auditorium was built in a Tudor style. However, walking into the entrance foyer, with its original hammer beam roof, stained glass windows, and ancient carved wooden screen, is a guaranteed smile-inducing experience.

Left: *The Red Lion Hotel in Milford Street was built at the same time as the cathedral, as the White Bear Inn, and substantial parts of the medieval structure have survived. It may be the longest running purpose-built hotel in the country.* © Richard Tambling

Bottom left: *The peaceful old courtyard of the Red Lion Hotel is one of Salisbury's hidden gems.* © Richard Tambling

Below: *The colourful Virginia creeper cladding the entire courtyard is thought to be over two hundred years old.*
© Richard Tambling

There is a lovely view of the cathedral from the peaceful and architecturally fascinating St Ann Street.

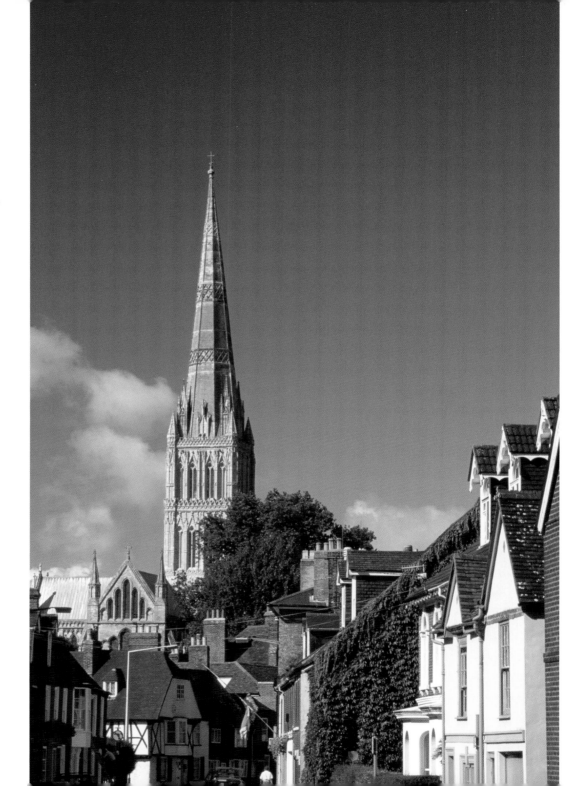

The medieval Joiners' Hall in St Ann Street is one of the best timber-framed buildings in the city. It is owned by the National Trust but is not open to the public. Its oriel windows are supported by rather grotesque and flamboyant carved figures. © Richard Tambling

The grand, classical portico of the White Hart Hotel still dominates St John's Street. A simple "White Hart" inn was completely rebuilt in 1790 to create a Regency-style coaching inn for rich tourists from London.

The fine, jettied gable of the King's Arms Hotel on St John's Street.

74

AROUND THE CITY

Nowhere is far from the city centre in Salisbury. It takes less than twenty minutes to stroll into the centre from the outskirts (much less on the Park and Ride buses), and the cathedral spire dominates the scene almost everywhere. Wherever you are the spire draws you in towards the Close like a moth to a lamp.

Sparkling, clear rivers with trout within, ducks upon and water voles beside are also your constant companion alongside car parks, shops and roads. Many of the streets radiating out from the city centre have interesting architectural features, as well as many shops, to distract and detain. A Victorian clock tower, standing close to the nineteenth century city boundary at the junction of Fisherton Street and Bridge Street, the distinctive old Salisbury General Infirmary, waterside walks, fascinating almshouses and old bridges with a rich history, all deserve to be appreciated.

Lower Bemerton, a quiet suburb lying just a short walk from the busy railway station, has two appealing churches and the air of a rural, sleepy village.

The landmark Victorian clock tower on Bridge Street sits atop remnants of the old city gaol.

© Richard Tambling

The rather severe brick façade of Salisbury General Infirmary now fronts a large residential complex.
Wiltshire's first infirmary, it was built in 1771 on land given by the Earl of Radnor, and was
much loved by staff and the people of Salisbury until it closed in 1993. © Richard Tambling

Left: *The River Avon flows through the heart of the city, past the old Infirmary's Victoria Nurses' Home, now luxury flats. The canalised channel has been softened by planting wild flowers.*

Fisherton Street was once separate from medieval Salisbury as the parish of Fisherton Anger. It is now a busy shopping street linking the city centre to the railway station.

80

Picturesque Ayleswade, or Harnham, Bridge spans the Avon south of the Close, not far from the ancient Aegel's Ford. It carried all Salisbury's southward-bound traffic until 1933. The tiny chapel of St John stands beside it, hidden inside a more modern house!

Left: *The delightful "Water Lane", originally a mill leat, is one of many waterside walks.*

Salisbury still has a number of functioning almshouses. Hussey's, off Castle Street, were founded in 1794, but the current buildings are Victorian. They flank a flower-filled courtyard, and have well modernised interiors.

© Richard Tambling

The hamlets of Fisherton Anger and Bemerton were gradually absorbed into the city as suburbs, but Lower Bemerton is still a relatively quiet, unspoilt spot. St John's church was built for the Pembrokes of Wilton.

St Andrew's in Lower Bemerton is a tiny chapel, seating only 30 people. It was built in the fourteenth century, and the building retains its original shape, but most of it has since been replaced. It features a medieval arch, and what is thought to be a 'leper's squint' in the south wall but is most famous for its association with the seventeenth-century poet and hymn writer George Herbert.

© Richard Tambling

THE ARTS AND LEISURE

Salisbury has a modern City Hall and Playhouse, a busy library, a charismatic Arts Centre, and what must be one of the most unusual cinemas in the country!

The Dean and Chapter of the cathedral have been very supportive of the Arts for many years. The prestigious annual Salisbury International Arts Festival, Saint George's Day events, sculpture exhibitions and concerts have taken place in the cathedral or in and around the Close, as well as at orthodox and unorthodox venues in and near the city. Even major firework displays have been staged within the Close.

Salisbury District Council and Wiltshire County Councils were also very supportive in past years so it is hoped that the new Wiltshire Council will continue to help Salisbury's reputation for spectacular performing and visual arts, and literary events to grow. Salisbury Festival spans two delicious weeks in May and June each year, but many extra events occur throughout the year. Highbrow, lowbrow, conventional or "challenging" delights are all on offer.

Salisbury offers great shopping opportunities for the dedicated shopaholic, with additional pleasant pedestrianised areas like the High Street and shopping malls at the Maltings, Cross Keys and Old George Mall.

Salisbury Playhouse, and its City Hall neighbour (below), might have had Prince Charles spitting feathers about their 1970s' architecture. The entertainment they each provide, however, is fortunately varied and often truly excellent.

© Richard Tambling

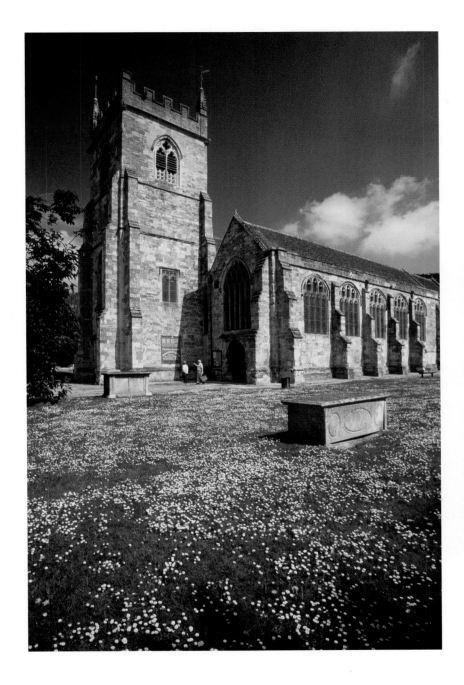

The church of St Edmund of Abingdon was much larger in medieval times, but was eventually made redundant as a place of worship. It has been given an innovative facelift and now serves as a busy, vibrant Arts Centre with a bar and café. A lively programme of performing arts, film festivals, exhibitions and art classes, all happens in a delightfully unique setting.

Reminders that the Arts Centre was once a church make it a fascinating secular venue. Stained glass windows, under a towering, vaulted roof, add to the atmosphere

Mephestomania's "Faust on Stilts" meets the Walking Madonna in the Close during a Salisbury Festival performance.

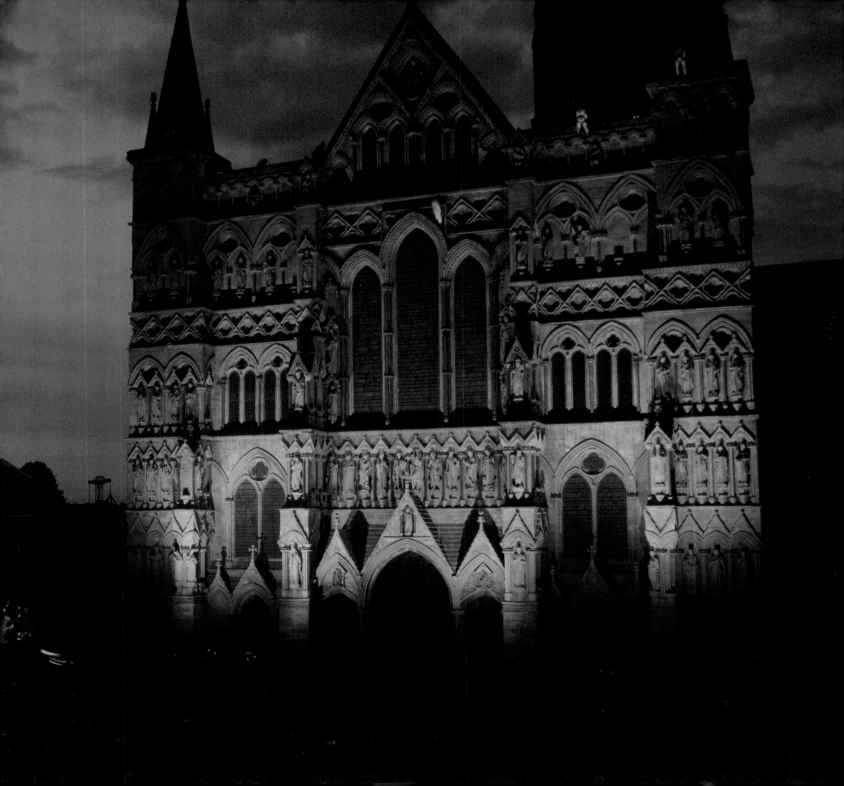

Anthony Gormley's "Field for the British Isles" temporarily enlivened the Cloisters during a sculpture exhibition.

Sophie Ryder's disturbing bronze "Minotaur and Hare" stood on the Cloister garth during a sculpture exhibition.

90

One of many spectacular firework displays in the Close.

Salisbury celebrates 23 April with Saint George's Day Festival activities. Saint George and his knights, but particularly the dragon, have appeared in many guises as they fight "out of town"…

…or in front of huge, enthusiastic crowds in the Market Square.

Salisbury's twelve foot tall giant is of uncertain, medieval origin. Adopted by the Guild of Tailors in the fifteen hundreds he has been known as Saint Christopher for several hundred years. Processional giants existed in several English cities, but only Salisbury's original has survived, making him unique. The giant, with Hob Nob, his hobby horse, now resides in Salisbury Museum and is well worth visiting. Any giants seen "out and about" are copies!

93

A side of Morris Dancers in Persil white attire entertains a crowd in the Market Square on Saint George's Day.

Dancers, colours and flags swirl during the Carnival Parade of one of Salisbury's Art Festivals.

94

Troops at Old Sarum await their call to fight!

Left: *The Maltings sits snugly beside a swan- and duck-filled River Avon, west of the Market Square. It is a very pleasant place to shop, despite its obvious modernity.*

Bottom left: *Old George Mall, a relatively modern shopping precinct, has a real buzz, especially on Saturdays. It is a place to meet friends and enjoy the "shopping experience"!*

© Richard Tambling

Below: *Salisbury has struggled over the years with traffic, and parking, in its narrow, medieval streets. Whether the pioneering Park and Ride system, with no fewer than five sites around the city, will help remains to be seen.*

SALISBURY'S
RURAL SETTING

Salisbury is at the confluence of four beautiful rivers, the Nadder, Avon, Wylye and Bourne, and the crystal clear Ebble joins them just south of the city. Otters, kingfishers and water voles live as secretive city residents or visitors. Water is ever present, and waterside walks abound. The rivers cut through rolling chalk downland all around the city. There are Local Nature Reserves near the Leisure Centre and at Bemerton. Salisbury has green areas in the Greencroft and the Maltings, and a huge open space, Hudson's Field, just below Old Sarum. There are well maintained formal parks on the west, north and east sides. Queen Elizabeth and Churchill Gardens, and Victoria Park are places to relax, paddle in the river, listen to concerts, walk the dog or meet friends. There is, of course, the green tranquility of the enormous Close. Long Bridge and the Town Path link the city with Harnham via the most charming of rural walks amidst fine old water-meadows. The views of the cathedral across the West Harnham water-meadows remain incredibly similar to those famously painted by Constable. The Britford water-meadows, just east of the city centre, are serene and lonely. The presence of these wet meadows, and the importance of the floodplain to a city with so much water flowing through its heart, has undoubtedly contributed to the relative lack of growth of the city's footprint.

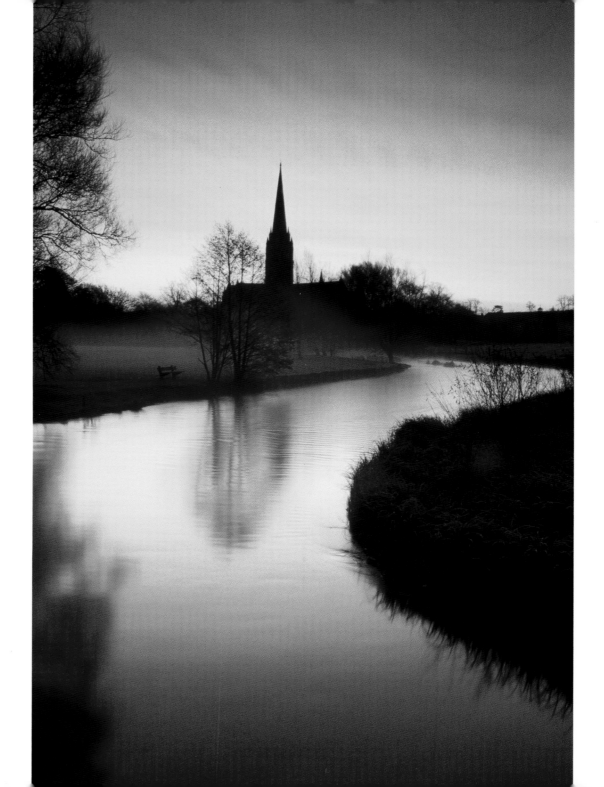

Cathedral and River Nadder at sunrise.

98

The iconic spire, seen from near Hole Farm on the Old Road, Alderbury.

The Avon flows through the tranquil Avon Valley Local Nature Reserve at the Butts, just twenty minutes' walk from the city centre. There is a brilliant, easy walk from here up to Old Sarum, via Stratford sub Castle.

Greencroft was the main communal open space in the medieval city. It was also the site of emergency plague burial pits and executions. Today it provides a pleasant, shady stroll back to the medieval chequers.

Formation kite flying at Hudson's Field, with Old Sarum in the background.

The verges of the ring road are awash with daffodils in spring. Churchill Gardens, beyond the fence, link the city to the Britford water-meadows.

Queen Elizabeth Gardens, flower-filled and immensely popular on sunny days, nestle between the city and the West Harnham water-meadows.

The cathedral, viewed in summer, across Queen Elizabeth Gardens from Long Bridge. This was a view made famous by Constable.

Severe flooding, every few winters in recent years, completely transforms the rivers and water-meadows. Salisbury and its cathedral were built on a massive floodplain.

Long Bridge at sunset.

106

The stroll along Town Path to the Old Mill at Harnham encompasses classic Constable scenery at any time of year. Almost all of the West Harnham water-meadows are owned or leased by the Harnham Water-meadows Trust. Members host guided walks across the meadows to enjoy the scenery and flowers, and to learn about the ongoing restoration of the water-meadow system.

Rose Cottage is a charming listed building owned by the Harnham Water-meadows Trust. It once housed the "drowner" of the water-meadows system but is now used as the Trust's education and information centre.

© Richard Tambling

A water mill already stood on the site of the Old Mill in 1135, but today's photogenic mill is of the 1500s. The brick building on the left was added in the 1800s. First a yarn factory, then a bone crushing mill then, right up until 1931, leased by a tallow candle maker. Thankfully, the Old Mill complex is now a charis-matic hotel, restaurant and bar, and the setting makes it well worth the stroll from town. The flint and ashlar chequered walls make a fine backdrop for ducks in the shallows, and for children leaping into the river on hot, summer days.

Cathedral from the Rose and Crown, Harnham.

110

The cathedral, particularly the spire, can be seen from all around the city.
Here, from across the water-meadows from Harnham.

The view across the water-meadows from the Grassmere House Hotel in Harnham.

The Britford water-meadows lie immediately east of the city.
The watercourse diverted from the Avon, was once important in the winter drowning of the grass.

The old eelhouse spans the river, whose meadows lie between Britford and the busy A36,
empty of people but home to swans, herons, kingfishers and marsh marigolds.

114

NORTH TO THE WOODFORD VALLEY

Driving north out of Salisbury through the pretty suburb of Stratford sub Castle, one passes through the probable site of the Roman town that lay below the western ramparts of Old Sarum. Beyond Stratford the River Avon has carved a lush, wooded valley, known as the Woodford valley. The picturesque villages of Lower, Middle and Upper Woodford sit quietly within the valley, on the western banks of the river, beside flowery, bird-filled water-meadows. There are two very different but excellent inns (the Wheatsheaf and the Bridge Inn) and a lovely old church to tempt the visitor. There are several peaceful spots to picnic by the clear waters of the Avon, and many delightful walks.

Heale House and Gardens, on the same side of the sheltered, tranquil valley, are steeped in history. The beautiful gardens, café and garden centre are well worth the four mile trip from the city centre.

Stratford sub Castle lies at the
northern edge of the city, and the
church of St Lawrence sits snugly in
the Avon valley, tucked below the
western ramparts of Old Sarum.

It has a medieval chancel, a
Gothic tower and flint and stone
chequerwork so typical of south
Wiltshire.

Stratford sub Castle post office closed back in the 1920s and is now a charming private home.

There are more fine water-meadows beside the Avon as it meanders sinuously down the Woodford valley, past Stratford sub Castle.

118

The pretty villages of Lower, Middle and Upper Woodford are strung out along the Avon's west bank, like pearls.

Heale House sheltered King Charles II before he fled to France. The house is private but the very attractive riverside gardens are open to the public all year.

119

The Japanese water garden at Heale features an eye-catching bridge.

The woodland walk is brightened by huge drifts of snowdrops in February.

EAST TO CLARENDON PALACE AND FIGSBURY RING

The Clarendon Way joining Old Sarum and Winchester, passes the dramatic ruins of the Palace of Clarendon on the way. The palace can be accessed on foot from Petersfinger on the eastern edge of Salisbury or from the attractive village of Pitton (where one can recover from one's exertions at the friendly Silver Plough). There were buildings on the site in Saxon or perhaps Norman times, and by the 1100s it was a regular, very important royal habitation, with a vast cellar known as "La Roche". It became the second royal palace to Westminster, and was popular as a hunting lodge, not least because of its totally enclosed deer park, the largest in medieval England.

This magnificent palace, had completely fallen out of favour by Elizabethan times, and the ruins were, until recently, a romantic tragedy of neglect, overgrown and hidden deep within woodland. It is one of the most significant medieval archaeological sites in Wiltshire, if not England. The site has now been cleared of ivy and woodland so that the splendour of its fascinating history can be appreciated. The layout of the Great Banqueting Hall, wine cellar and other buildings, with information boards, help show just how important this palace and its hunting park were. The landscape and setting are fantastic but it is still one of the best kept secrets in Wiltshire! It is certainly a place to explore, and share with the grazing llamas.

A track leading up to a substantial hillfort lies just east of Salisbury, signposted off the A30 London Road. The sound of singing skylarks fills the air as one enjoys views back to the cathedral spire and towards Salisbury Plain from the high circular ramparts of Figsbury Ring. This splendid causewayed camp or enclosure, owned by the National Trust, is ablaze with bright orchids and other downland flowers throughout the summer months. Its steep slopes are also home to good numbers of butterflies such as stunning Adonis and Chalkhill Blues.

121

The nine-metre high surviving fragment of the northeast wall of the Great Hall of Clarendon Palace in its neglected, but romantic, state. It has more recently been given a dramatic makeover.

The sound of singing skylarks fills the air as one enjoys views back to the cathedral spire from the high circular ramparts of Figsbury Ring. This splendid, Neolithic causewayed camp or enclosure, owned by the National Trust, is ablaze with bright orchids and colourful butterflies throughout the summer months.

A lipstick pink pyramidal orchid on the outer banks.

124

SOUTH TO THE AVON
AND EBBLE VALLEYS

The River Avon flows south from Salisbury, beside the A338 Downton Road in a broad valley. Longford Castle sits in splendid isolation next to the Avon, in a private 250 acre park that is part of the Longford Estate.

Heading further down the A338, the little village of Charlton All Saints is a good starting point for an enjoyable walk on a public footpath that crosses the water-meadows then the River Avon via Standlynch Weir and through woodland next to the magnificent Trafalgar House in its private parkland setting.

Turning back towards Salisbury then west off the A338 by Bodenham, a tiny back road meanders through several sleepy villages in the Ebble valley. Nunton, Odstock and Homington delight the eye, and may cause one to tarry at the Radnor Arms or Yew Tree Inn, before one reaches a picture postcard crossroads by the Fox and Goose in Coombe Bissett, on the A354 Blandford Road. The back road then follows the route of the Ebble into tiny Stratford Tony, with its thirteenth-century church and nearby Roman ford. There is breathtaking scenery along much of this route.

Longford Castle was completed in 1591, on a mystical triangular plan, with broad, round towers at the three corners, and extensive parkland beside the Avon. It has been altered over the centuries by a long succession of owners, but has kept its fairytale castle appearance. It is now the seat of the 9th Earl of Radnor. Grand formal gardens were laid out in 1832.

126

The weir at Standlynch, just south of Longford Castle, stands on a beautiful, ponderous stretch of the Avon, close to the little village of Charlton All Saints.

Trafalgar Park, originally known as Standlynch House, was given to Admiral Lord Nelson's brother, by "the Nation", in gratitude for the Battle of Trafalgar. The current owner hosts wonderful operatic evenings, and offers Trafalgar Park as an idyllic setting for weddings and conferences.

The neatly-chequered Standlynch church sits close to the Avon, far below the house. Now, after many years of disuse, it is once again part of the Trafalgar Park estate, and may be restored. There are several interesting Nelson family graves in the churchyard.

The lush, tranquil Ebble valley lies south of the city. Grazing cattle are deaf to the shrill piping of electric blue kingfishers seen here regularly.

The old water-meadows still have their sluices and "carriers".

Odstock's solid medieval church of St Mary stands close to the crystal clear, babbling Ebble.

The River Ebble passes pretty cottages and the welcoming Fox and Goose Inn as it flows through the heart of Coombe Bissett.

Beautiful examples of thatched cottages, with chequered flint and ashlar walls,
abound in south Wiltshire's river valley villages, as here in Coombe Bissett.

Another attractive thatched cottage nestles beside the Ebble in the tiny village of Stratford Tony.
One of four Roman roads from Old Sarum crosses the river close by.

WEST TO WILTON

Heading west out of Salisbury, via the suburb of Harnham, one passes Netherhampton, a village hardly any larger now than a hundred years ago. Having just 50 or so houses and a good pub, the Victoria and Albert, it lies between Salisbury and the high walls of the Wilton estate, on a tranquil loop road next to the River Nadder, home to otters, kingfishers and water voles.

A short distance further west up another little back road, Salisbury Racecourse, in its idyllic setting on the downs close to Netherhampton, is small and very intimate. Many local families take a picnic and spend an evening at the races in summer.

A little west again, Wilton sits next to the wonderful, clear River Wylye. It was once the capital of Saxon Wiltonshire and has, amazingly, kept much of its Saxon street plan. It steadily became a shrinking violet as Salisbury grew in stature and power but is, today, a smart, friendly little town. Just fifteen minutes from Salisbury, it boasts a flamboyant Italianate church and the truly magnificent Wilton House, stately home of the Earls of Pembroke. The Wilton garden centre, church ruins, almshouses and the Wilton Shopping Village are all attractions, and Wilton is, of course, world famous for its Wilton carpets.

Netherhampton, nestling beside the Nadder, has resisted becoming a city suburb.
St Catherine's church has the chequered walls typical of the area.

136

Netherhampton House has a striking façade that conceals a much earlier cottage.
It served as a boarding school for boys in the nineteenth century.

Salisbury Racecourse is one of England's oldest flat racing courses. Racing has been taking place on (or probably near!) its scenic downland venue since the sixteenth century. It is small, friendly and absolutely the perfect setting for a summer evening's racing and picnic. © Richard Tambling

The ruined nave of St Mary stands alongside the market square, in Wilton.

It is a slightly bizarre experience to suddenly catch sight of Wilton's flamboyant, Italian Romanesque, basilica-like church of St Mary and St Nicholas for the first time! It has a tall, isolated campanile and wildly extravagant interior…

…and a large Rose window.

Saint John's Priory almshouses. Saint John's Square has been much altered but there have been almshouses here since 1135.

Wilton House stands on the site of a Saxon nunnery and is undoubtedly one of Britain's most magnificent stately homes. The attractive parkland setting has cedars of Lebanon and a beautiful old oak, struck by lightning.

The River Wylye crosses the estate and the Nadder flows beneath the gorgeous Palladian bridge, setting for romantic summer concerts.

The site of the old carpet factory in Wilton has been transformed into a popular, bustling shopping centre.

The Wilton Royal Carpet Factory was granted its royal charter by William III in 1699. The company is still making high quality carpets today but, sadly, the factory no longer offers tours.

144